The Family
Camping Guide

By
Greg Robinson

TABLE OF CONTENTS

The Family Camping Guide

Introduction

Do you love the outdoors? Do you feel like you never get enough time to really spend outside? Then you should take the family camping for a family vacation this year. Going camping as a family can be a great way to spend some quality time with each other and make memories that will last a lifetime. You might even start a family tradition that your kids will carry on with their own children.

By nature kids love to get outside and play, and these days not enough kids go outside to play on a regular basis. Overly structured schedules, parents that work, daycare, and safety concerns all mean that kids usually end up indoors most of the time in front of the computer, video game console or TV.

Because kids love the outdoors and don't really get that much of an opportunity to spend a lot of time outside a vacation spent enjoying a national park or hiking through a forest can be a great way to get kids off the couch and doing something more active.

There are lots of different destinations that you can use to plan a family camping trip. National parks are a great place to take the family camping and they are usually fairly inexpensive too. Or you can go somewhere exotic and plan a camping vacation as a way to really explore somewhere that you wouldn't otherwise get to see.

Camping vacations also usually cost less than other types of vacations so if you're trying to save money or you don't have the money to take an expensive family vacation this year a camping trip across the country or even to a local park can be a fun way to get time with the family that doesn't cost a lot of money.

When you start to plan a family camping vacation it might seem overwhelming because there are a lot of details that you need to think about in order to make the trip a success. What gear to use, which gear is the best, what food do you need to bring, and of course, where should you go are all questions that you will need to answer before you can have a successful family camping trip.

Planning a family camping vacation can be a lot of work, but it's worth the effort. Your kids will only be kids for so long, and a family camping trip is a great way to make memories that will last a lifetime.

The Five Best Reasons to Go Camping as a Family

Not convinced that camping is right for your family or that a few days or a week spent in the wilderness without the distraction of TV or video games is the ideal family vacation? These five reasons will convince you that a family camping trip is the idea vacation. You should go camping as a family because:

1. It's educational – The kids will learn about nature and wildlife as well as about learning about national monuments and state parks. Kids also learn other skills from camping like independence, self-reliance, wilderness skills and first aid.

2. It's active- Obesity is a growing epidemic among children. Instead of taking your kids to a theme park or taking them on a vacation where they will just sit around most of them time taking them camping will be encouraging them to swim, hike, and do other outdoor activities.

3. It's a way to get great quality time – When you're off on a family camping trip you will have lots of quality time to spend with your spouse and your kids because it will just be the family in a quiet, beautiful outdoor environment. No TV, videogames, movies, or other distractions will keep you from focusing on your family or keep them from focusing on you. For families where both parents work and are busy all the time it's a wonderful way to reconnect with your kids.

4. It's cheap – Most camping vacations cost a lot less than traditional vacations. Camping in state parks or other historical areas often costs less than $100 for a week's worth of camping. You will need to spend money on gear, but later in the book we'll look at ways you can cut the costs of buying camping gear.

The biggest expenses that you will have will be food and gas. Eating meals that you cook yourself with groceries you bring with you will be much cheaper than eating in a restaurant three times a day like you would on a traditional vacation, and gas will probably be cheaper than what you would spend on airfare for the whole family.

5. It's something everyone in the family can enjoy – Wouldn't it be nice to be able to relax and enjoy yourself without having to listen to one child complain that he or she wants to go to the pool while another cries bitterly because you won't buy them a new boat/sweater/ toy or trinket and the other just sits in the corner with a sullen look and kicks the bed repeatedly?

A camping vacation is a real vacation for the whole family because there is always something fun and active to do for people who want to do something active and that leaves plenty of time for the people that want to do nothing (usually the parents) to sit and enjoy the quiet stillness of nature.

Ten Great Family Camping Vacation Ideas

When you're thinking about planning a great family camping vacation the first thing that you need to do is pick out a destination. National parks and other historical sites are always a good choice as the destination for a family camping trip but you usually need to reserves spots pretty far in advance because during tourist season in the summer the available camping spots tend to fill up pretty fast.

Here are ten great family camping destinations that you might want to consider when you're planning a family camping vacation.

1. Local Parks

If you want to have all the fun of a family camping vacation without going too far from home you can look online for any state parks that are within a day's drive of where you live. Local parks that are within a day's drive are great when you are camping with small children because if they are too frightened or if for some reason you need to take them home you're not too far away from home.

Also, if you have pets, or if you regularly take care of a sick family member and you would feel more comfortable being closer to home a local park can be a good way to still get to take a family vacation.

2. Yellowstone National Park

Yellowstone National Park is a very popular family camping spot. This massive national park touches three states: Montana, Wyoming, and Idaho. Yellowstone is famous for Old Faithful, one of the longest running geysers, as well as a collection of other geysers and hot springs. Wildlife is abundant in Yellowstone Park and you can and the kids can see wolves, bison, grizzly bears, and elk as well as smaller wildlife species.

There are endless activities to keep the kids busy including some of the best hiking in the country. There are restaurants and stores near the park if you want a restaurant meal or run out of supplies but you'll probably be too busy having fun in the park to want to leave it.

Camping at Yellowstone is very cheap. Basic campsites that have almost no amenities are only $12 per night. Campsites that offer flush toilets, showers and other amenities on site are only $18.50 per night. There is a $25 per vehicle fee plus $12 per person that you will have to pay to get into the park but that will be that fee covers seven days of visiting the park.

Overall, camping at Yellowstone is a huge value, especially when you consider the beautiful scenery and all the free activities that you will have access to. Fires are permitted in special fire grates so you can have that all important family campfire at night.

3. Crater of Diamonds State Park

For a really exciting family adventure take a family camping vacation at Crater of Diamonds State Park in Arkansas. Crater of Diamonds Park is the only diamond producing site in the world that allows the public to come in, camp, and go digging for diamonds. You even get to keep any diamonds that you might find. Visitors to the park have found many different types and sizes of diamonds but the diamonds that are most often found are white, brown and yellow diamond.

You can bring your own diamond hunting equipment with you if you want, but nothing that is motorized or has wheels. Making sifting screens at home is easy and cheap and a great art project for the kids. Also bring a few buckets and a few shovels or trowels, and definitely bring some gloves. If you don't want the hassle of bringing your own equipment you can rent buckets, shovels, and sifting screens at the park for less than $10.

There are lots of other types of rocks to be found at Crater of Diamonds Park too. Visitors can find lamproite, amethyst, banded agate, jasper, peridot, garnet, quartz, calcite, barite and hematite, among others. Best of all, any precious stones or diamonds that you find on the site are yours to keep, even if they are large and valuable! The kids will love prospecting for diamonds and other stones, but there are also acres of land that are great for hiking and other activities.

Camping at the Crater of Diamonds Park is very inexpensive. Campsite fees are less than $20 and include bathroom facilities, showers and laundry facilities. The campground facility also has a nearly 15,000-ft water park and playground that the kids will love and admission is less than $6 per person, less than $4 per child. The water playground is also available for private rental with lifeguards on duty so if you want to rent the water park for a child's birthday you can.

Want to check out the local wildlife while you're there? The park has a specially built secluded blind where campers can go and sit and watch turkeys and other local wildlife in the wild. It's a great way to let your kids get close to some real wildlife without them or the wildlife getting scared. Getting to see wild animals in their natural habitat from that close of a distance is a huge treat for little kids that love animals.

Crater of Diamonds Park is a fabulous place for an inexpensive but very fun family camping vacation. You can hike, swim, camp, and dig for diamonds so that the kids will never get bored. And who knows, you might find some great diamonds or other precious stones that you can have made into jewelry so that you'll always have souvenirs from that family camping trip.

Make reservations early though, because the campground only has 59 camp sites and they fill up fast. You can make reservations online or over the phone with a credit card.

4. The Grand Canyon

The Grand Canyon is a national treasure that everyone should see at least one. Your child could come away from a family trip to the Grand Canyon with memories that will last a lifetime. Grand Canyon National Park is in Arizona, and sees thousands of visitors from around the world every year.

There are plenty of activities to keep family members of all ages busy in the Grand Canyon. You can take a donkey ride down into the actual canyon from the top, which is an amazing experience. You can also go out on the relatively recently build Skywalk. The Skywalk is an engineering marvel that was competed in 2004. It's a bridge made entirely of glass and perched on the edge of the Canyon, overlooking the Colorado River.

The Skywalk is built in a horseshoe shape so you can walk out over the Canyon, and then walk back to land in one loop. You can see below you as well as above you thanks to the glass. Not for those with a dread fear of height, obviously, but a unique opportunity for those who can deal with the feeling of being suspended over the canyon. Admission to the Skywalk is free with a valid park admission sticker and you can spend as long as you like gazing down into the Canyon.

There are also three Indian reservations near the Canyon so if you want to take an educational and interesting day trip while you're there you can head over to the Navajo Reservation, the Hualapai Reservation, or the Havasupai Reservation.

Hiking is also a popular activity in the Grand Canyon. There are plenty of hiking trails that are appropriate for the whole family but you should stay away from the backcountry hiking if you are hiking with kids, unless you and they are extremely experienced hikers. Even the best hikers find backcountry hiking in the Grand Canyon challenging because of the extreme heat and the extreme cold at night, the complete lack of water, and the effects of being so far from civilization or help, if it was needed. If you really want to brave the backcountry you should consider going on a guided day hike instead of going it alone.

There is a $25 fee per vehicle for entrance to the park, separate from the camping fees. There are two campgrounds for Grand Canyon National Park, one on each rim of the Canyon. Campsite prices are $18-20 for campsites with water and electricity hookups, showers, laundry facilities and bathrooms and $12 for campsites with fewer amenities.

The campsites are open all year round. If you want to visit the Grand Canyon when there aren't thousands of other tourists there you might want to plan your family camping vacation for sometime other than busy summer months. Temperatures in the winter are still quite mild.

5. Everglades National Park

Florida is known for being a great vacation destination for families. Seaworld, Disney World, and the Universal Theme Park are all well known family vacation spots. But you might not know that Florida also has some great family camping, all over the state, with lots of fun things to see and do that don't cost a fortune, like camping in Everglades National Park.

Everglades National Park is the best subtropical wilderness reserve in the US. You can see all kinds of wildlife in the park including American crocodile, Florida panther, and West Indian manatees. The park covers more than a million acres, so plan on spending at least a week there if you can so that you can really get the full experience that the Park has to offer.

Kayaking and canoeing, along with fishing, are the major water activities the park has to offer. You can explore Florida Bay, Whitewater Bay, and the Ten Thousand Islands by kayak or canoe, and you can fish there too. There is no better way to explore the Everglades with the kids than by kayak or canoe, they will love it.

Hiking is also great for families in the Everglades National Park. Trails are clearly marked and most trails are smooth, suitable for bicycles or foot traffic, and easy enough that even small children can walk then without getting exhausted. Ask at the park visitors centers for maps of hiking trails.

Camping in the park can be done at one of three sites that

are adjacent to the park. These sites are $14 per night and have limited amenities but do have bathrooms and showers. Fires are permitted in fire grates. There is a $10 charge per vehicle to enter the park, and that admission ticket is good for 7 days.

There are various guided tours that you can go on in the park or you can take a map and strike out on your own. Most families prefer to do a mixture of guided tours, such as the Shark Bay tour, and individual explorations throughout the park.

Unless you are an experienced camper, you should avoid the wet season, May through November. Temperatures reach average highs of 90° F, with humidity over 90%, and a heat index of over 100 F. Afternoon thunderstorms can be expected daily with heavy rainfalls, making conditions very difficult. However, it also means the park is nearly empty with great opportunities for solitude. There are fewer park services available these months.

6. Denali National Park

Not every family is going to want to make the trek to Alaska for a family vacation but if you want a vacation that is exotic and far away without having to travel too far then Alaska might be just perfect for you. Even though Alaska is in the U.S. it feels like it's worlds away from the rest of the country because of the breathtaking scenery and splendor that encompasses that state.

Denali National Park and Preserve covers more than 6

million acres, including a portion of Mt. McKinley, the highest peak in the U.S. The park it broken down into three sections: Denali National Park, Denali Wilderness, and the Denali Preserve. Hunting is prohibited in the Wilderness but is allowed under certain conditions in the other sections of the park.

There are lot of activities to keep you and the family busy in the park, and close to the park. Hiking is the main activity, with trails ranging from those easy enough for very small children to tougher back country trails that aren't appropriate for young children or inexperienced hikers. Wildlife is extremely abundant and you can expect to see wolves, bears, caribou, moose and smaller animals like ground squirrels. You can also find dozens of species of birds include eagles, raptors, owls, ravens, plovers, gyrfalcons and more. At last count more than 157 species had been sighted in Denali National Park.

Guided tours and demonstrations are happening daily in the park and you and the kids can have a great time watching a dog sled demonstration and learning about this uniquely Alaskan mode of travel. You can get a ride on a dog sled too. You can also take guided hikes and tours around famous Horseshoe Lake, or walk through the Alaskan frozen tundra with a native guide.

If you and your family like to snowshoe or cross country ski then a vacation to Denali can be a dream come true. Spend days dog sledding or skiing and nights in a traditional igloo or "camp" at one of nearby lodges. Want to see the best possible views of this stunning glacial park? Then head to the nearby areas and book a flightseeing tour, where a small plane or helicopter ride will give you the most amazing views of Mt. McKinley and Denali National Park that you could ever dream of.

Camping at Denali National Park is a little bit different than at other national parks. You need to stay at a lodge, and the prices of the lodges vary depending on the season that you go. You will also need to pay for shuttle service to and from the park from the closest airport, which is in Anchorage. A National Parks Pass that you will need to get into the park costs $50, but it good for 12 months and will also get you into any other national parks that you want to visit during those 12 months.

7. The Appalachian Trail

The Appalachian Trail is a national treasure that makes a great family camping trip. The trail itself is over 2,000 miles long and goes through Georgia, North Carolina, Tennessee, Virginia, West Virginia, Maryland, Pennsylvania, New Jersey, New York, Connecticut, Massachusetts, Vermont, New Hampshire, and Maine. An international addition to the trail runs through Canada to the North Atlantic Ocean.

Many people have tried to hike the entire trail in one shot camping along the way but only a tiny fraction have made it. Because the trail covers a wide expanse of territory the terrain of the trail ranges from easy meadow hiking to extremely difficult mountain hiking.

The trail is marked with clear markers throughout its length. You can camp in tents along the trail or your can stay in three sided lean-tos that are provided at regular intervals to give hikers a chance to sleep in a sturdy shelter. There are usually cleared spots to pitch a tent close to the shelter and there are always clean water sources and outhouses near by as well. These shelters are maintained entirely by volunteers; there are no paid staff that work on the trail at all.

The AT, as it's known, also crosses several towns along the way so that hikers can stop and get supplies, a shower, do some laundry, and get a hot restaurant meal. The trail is entirely free from beginning to end, making it a very low cost family camping destination.

Since it's pretty likely that you won't be able to, and probably won't want to, hike the entire trail what you can do is mark off a portion of the trail that you do want to hike and make travel arrangements into the area of the trail that you want to start at and out of the area that you want to end at. Starting and ending at one of the little towns that the trail crosses is a smart thing to do because then you can arrange for a taxi to take you to town where you can make arrangement to get back home.

Hiking the AT is a great family vacation but it's not really appropriate for younger children, so if you have young children you might want to wait until they are a little older to take a camping vacation on the Appalachian Trail. Since the terrain can get rough and you do need to cover a certain amount of distance to get to a town it's better if you wait until you're sure the kids are up to the challenge before you take them out on the trail.

8. Yosemite National Park

Yosemite National Park in California is known around the world for its stunning waterfalls and sheer granite cliffs. If you and your family enjoy rock climbing then Yosemite National Park is a great destination for you. The park itself is more than 200,000 acres although most people don't see more than about 10 miles of that because there are so many things to do and see in the park.

The sheer granite cliffs and stunning waterfalls are remnants of a glacier that carved the cliffs and waterfalls out of the Sierra mountains millions of years ago. Most of the waterfalls are fed by melting snow from the mountains. Because the water is coming from the mountains during the late summer and early fall the waterfalls are often bare because there has been no snowfall but by early winter they are flowing once again. Yosemite Falls, the highest waterfall in North America, is the crowing jewel of the many waterfalls in the park.

Hike up into the Sierra Mountains and you can spend the day in one of the beautiful mountain meadows that are scattered throughout the park. You can hike on the flat, grassy land, or enjoy the beautiful scenery with a picnic. There are several small glaciers in the park so you and the kids can enjoy the experience of seeing and even walking up to a real glacier that is a miniature version of the glacier that created the Yosemite Valley.

When it comes to getting around the park you can hike, bike, ski (in appropriate areas) or go on horseback. Take a guided horseback tour into the mountains to see all the best views without having to take a strenuous mountain hike or if you have little ones with you that can't make the hard hike into the mountains.

The entrance fee to get into the park is $20 per car, there is a smaller fee for those that come in on bicycles or horseback. Campgrounds at Yosemite National Park fill up quickly so plan to make a reservation well in advance if you want to plan a camping trip to the park. The campgrounds all have flush toilets, dump stations, showers and laundry facilities. Prices range from $10-$20 per day depending on the campground and the season.

9. Glacier National Park

Glacier National Park in Montana is a spectacular place to take a family camping trip. More than 50 glaciers can be found in the park, and more than 200 lakes and streams. The hiking is great and very family friendly in this park. There are more than 730 miles of marked hiking trails in the million acre park.

When you're entering the park you have to drive down the Going To the Sun Road. It's a 50 mile road that cuts right across the heart of park and hugs a glacier in some sections. It's an amazing drive that the kids are sure to find impressive.

The road is a National Historic Landmark and is often mentioned as a feat of modern engineering, even though it was completed in 1932. Before that time visitors would arrive by boat or take a train into the heart of the park. Once you're in the park you will be amazed by the beautiful scenery, the abundant wildlife and the glaciers.

The land that the park sits on was once the home of two powerful Indian tribes, the Blackfoot and Kootenai. Many of the spots that were considered sacred to these tribes are still intact and are marked so that you will know when you are coming up on ground that these tribes thought were special and important. You can also find historical information about those tribes in the towns near the park if you want to take the time to teach your kids more about Native American history.

Because of the lush grasses, abundance of water and great location the park is teeming with wildlife. When you're out hiking you could come across bears, elk, moose, mountain goats, deer, wolves, bobcats, lynxes, wolverines, mink, foxes and coyotes.

Camping in Glacier State Park is a little bit different than camping in other parks. Because of the elevation and because of the glaciers the temperature gets close to freezing just about every night. So it's important that when you're going camping in Glacier State Park you bring plenty of warm clothes and cold weather gear. Even though the weather gets very warm and beautiful during the day it's best to be prepared for quick temperature changes because of the variety of the landscape.

There are ten campgrounds for visitors in the park, plus a special section of campsites in the back country for experienced hikers that want to try some back country hiking. Some of the campgrounds have showers, bathrooms, laundry facilities and a market with limited supplies but only two or three of the ten have those amenities. Those fill up fast, so make reservations early, at least 6 months in advance. Campsites in the park range from $10-$20 per day depending on where they are and what amenities they offer.

10. Volcano National Park

A family camping trip to Volcano National Park in Hawaii is a great way to experience what Hawaii is like without spending a lot of money. There are two active volcanoes within the park, and they are two of the most active volcanoes in the world. There are lots of exciting things to see and do inside the park, including seeing the unique formations left by the lava and hiking up to the top of one of the active volcanoes.

Other activities that are appropriate for all ages in the park include hiking through the park, interactive exhibits and displays about volcanoes, lectures and presentations like "After Dark in the Park," a nightly presentation of topics related to Hawaiian native culture and other cultural exhibits and presentations. There is a lot more to see inside Volcano National Park besides the volcanoes. The wildlife in the park is amazing because the park is in a tropical rainforest, the only one in U.S. territory. There are thousands of species of plants, birds, and other animals. You can also visit sea turtles and other wildlife in their natural habitat, experience a little bit of native Hawaiian culture and relax in the glorious tropical weather of Hawaii.

It's recommended that if you want to hike up to the volcano craters or get close to the volcanoes that you join a ranger-led hike. There are some special safety precautions that you will need to use hiking close to an active volcano so going on a pre-selected path with an experienced guide will make sure that your family stays safe. There are guided volcano hikes offered for free at regular intervals so it shouldn't be hard to find one that fits into your schedule.

Back country hiking in Volcano National Park is by permit only, so if you and your family want to camp or even hike out in the wilds of the park you will need to stop by the Visitor Center and register for a permit before you go. This is for your own safety and so that the park rangers know how many people are out hiking in the back country at any given point of time. Permits are free.

There is a $10 entrance fee per vehicle to get into the park. That admission fee will get you into the park for seven days so you won't need to pay another admission fee if you leave the park and return another day. In Volcano National Park there are no other fees. Campsites are free, and are first come first serve so if you want to get a good campsite you need to stake a claim for your site as soon as you get to the park.

There aren't a lot of amenities on site when camping in Volcano National Park but the nearby town has laundry facilities, a market, a nice choice of restaurants and some reasonably priced hotels and bed and breakfasts if you decide that you need at least one night in a hotel. Because a trip to Hawaii involves more travel than a lot of other national parks often families will arrive and stay in a hotel the first night while they regroup and gather their gear for the actual camping part of the trip.

What You Need to Know About Camping in National Parks

Camping is a little different at each national park, and each national park has its own specific rules and regulations. When you call to get more information about camping at a particular park make sure that you find out these things:

What amenities are offered at each campsite?

Often the campsites at a national park with have different amenities. Some with have things like flush toilets, showers, laundry facilities, a market, or a swimming pool and play area. Some campsites will have space for RVs and trailers and will have water and electricity hookups that you can use. Others will not. Make sure you ask ahead of time what amenities are available at each site so that if you need to make reservations at another campground that has better amenities you can.

How much does a space cost and how many people does that include?

Most national park campsites cost between $10 and $20 per night for up to six people. If you have a large family or if you are traveling with friends or neighbors and their families you will have to ask what the group campsite rate is to make sure that you have a realistic idea of what camping at that park will cost. You should also find out what the entrance fee to the park is.

Are fires allowed?

Most national parks will allow you to have small campfires and cooking fires in specially designed fire grates or fire pits. But some parks have very strict rules about when fires can be lit, and some parks that have a problem with forest fires might not permit fires during certain months when forest fires can be a problem. Find out what the rules are about having a fire before you go.

Are firearms allowed?

If you plan on doing some hunting on your vacation you will need to find out in advance what the park's rules are about firearms. If you're going to be doing a lot of back country hiking or hunting some parks, like Denali National Park in Alaska, will allow small firearms. However most national parks do not allow firearms of any kind, so check to be sure.

What permits do you need?

This is a very important question to ask. Some parks require campers to have special permits based on the number of people that are camping. Others want you to have a permit based on the amount of days that you will be camping. All national parks will require that you have an entrance pass. Find out in detail exactly what permits you will need and what information you will have to bring in order to get them so that you're prepared when you get to the park.

Are reservations allowed?

Some national parks will take reservations but others won't. Typically the ones that do allow reservations will let you make reservations online or on the phone with a credit card. You can reserve a spot for your entire stay.

Reserved spots fill up very quickly so it's recommended that you make reservations at the national park of your choice at least six months if not a year ahead of time. If a campground does fill up with reservations you can add your name to a waiting list, there are usually at least a few last minute cancellations but that can make planning a vacation difficult.

The majority of the campgrounds at national parks are first come, first serve. That means in order to get a good campsite you need to arrive at the park very early in the morning and it doesn't hurt to arrive early in the season or late in the season too.

Typically the parks are the most crowded during late June and July. Traffic in August usually tapers off as families get ready for a new school year. If you can plan a vacation during a time other than that hectic summer season you will probably have a better chance of getting a great campsite.

Whether you can't get reservations or you arrive too late in the day to get a good campsite it's always a good idea to have a map to the nearest town and the number of a few hotels in the area. Travel plans usually go awry and you might end up needing to spend a night in a local hotel so that you can arrive at the park bright and early the next morning to get a good campsite.

Is there a dump station?

If the camping ground doesn't have a dump station, be prepared to carry your trash away with you to the nearest local dump or camping dump station. Back country campsites and other isolated sites might not have dump facilities, but most campgrounds that are well populated or within easy access of a main road do have dump stations so that getting rid of your trash won't be a problem. But it's still a good idea to find out in advance if the campground you're planning on staying at has a dump station.

When you're camping in national parks, just like when you're camping other places, remember to be courteous and respectful of other campers and when you're not sure what the rules are ask a park ranger or ask at the Visitor Information booth. Every park has a Visitor Information booth or building where you can register and get information.

Five Tips for Choosing a Great Campsite

Finding a great campsite can be tricky. You need to be ready to pounce when you find one and you also need to be well connected and know where to look to find the best family – friendly ones. Here are five tips you can use to help you find a great family friendly campsite.

1. Ask around – Word of mouth is the best way to find a great campsite. Ask other parents and family and friends that like to go camping where they had good experiences and where they had bad ones so that you can avoid those places. Most of the time people are happy to talk about the campsites they would and wouldn't recommend.

2. Scour the Internet – Go onto some family camping forums or parents websites and do a little digging to find out what campsites and campgrounds other parents really liked. Remember that you should take everything that you read online with a grain of salt, but if you read between the lines you should be able to get a pretty good idea of which places are good and which ones aren't.

3. Research before you go – While you're online go to the websites of a few campgrounds to view photos of the site before you go there. Some campgrounds have fully interactive websites with virtual tours and lots of information about the amenities they have. Some other sites make dig around the site to find the information that you're looking for but if you look hard enough you can usually tell if a site is family friendly or not by the photos and language on the website.

4. Be flexible with your vacation dates – If you find a great campground that seems perfect for a family camping trip but they are all booked up during the period that you want to go it's worth changing your plans. Being flexible about the dates that you're willing to travel can make the difference between spending your family camping vacation at a great campsite or spending it trapped at a bad campsite having a miserable time. Remember, if your kids aren't having fun neither will you.

5. Share – If the great campground that a friend recommended is full but your friends have a site ask if you can share their campsite or ask them if they would be willing to split the time with you. If your families are close then a joint vacation with a shared campsite might be a lot of fun for everyone.

If your friends do agree to share the campsite make sure that you pay for the half fees and be willing to pitch in and do a little more than your share of the chores because they will be doing you a big favor. A little consideration when camping with others will go a long way towards the making the trip more pleasant for everyone.

Five Amenities to Look for in a Campground or Campsite

Everyone has a different level of comfort when it comes to camping. You and your family might be totally comfortable "roughing it' with very few amenities or you might consider it "roughing it" to not be staying anywhere near a spa. When you're going camping with the family you need to think about what amenities are going to make life easier with the kids around.

You might not mind having to haul water from a community spigot a half mile away but when you have to do it with a toddler in tow three or four times a day then you might think it's a pain. Even if you have liked "roughing it" in the past if you have children that are camping with you then you definitely should consider finding a campground with these amenities to make your vacation and theirs more fun.

1. Bathroom facilities – Using outhouses or pit toilets might be fun for the kids but when it comes to sanitation and keeping kids clean they are no fun at all. If your kids are older they will probably not want to use anything but a regular flush toilet, and if you have little ones you will want to be around a proper bathroom with plenty of hot water and soap.

2. Showers – Going more than a day, or two at a stretch, without a hot shower is no fun and not relaxing. Make sure that you bring flip flops to wear in the shower and make sure that you check out the cleanliness of the shower before you go in but having a shower on site should be a must for any campground.

3. Dump station for trash – Unless you want to end up having trash with you throughout your vacation and having to carry it out of the park or campground with you check to be sure that there is a dump station or trash dumping ground on site.

4. Electricity and water hookups – This is really only important if you're camping in an RV but if you are planning on using your RV as a place to shower, cook, and relax you will need electricity and water hook ups. Not every RV campground offers them to double check before you reserve a campsite.

5. A pool, playground or community center. No matter how great all that family together time is eventually you and the kids are going to need some time apart. As long as the

campground has a pool or a playground you can send the kids off to find some other kids to play with for awhile. Just make sure if it's a pool that there are lifeguards are duty.

If the campground has a community center often they will have video games, computers, TVs and DVD players so the kids can hang out there during the day for awhile and you can meet up with some other parents there at night.

Ten Signs of a Family Friendly Campground

Some campgrounds will advertise themselves as being family friendly but some don't because they don't want to alienate campers without kids. However, if you are going to be camping with your kids it's important that you choose a family-friendly campground because you don't want to end up at a campsite next to a surly person or couple that hates kids when yours are going to be running around playing and making noise.

If you're not sure if a campground is family friendly or not look for a few of these ten signs of a family friendly campground. If a campsite has three or more of these signs then you and your kids will probably have a lot of fun there:

1. The campground hosts kids' activities. If you see signs at the campground or information on the website about junior rangers programs for kids, or arts and crafts classes in the community center, or junior hiking programs and so on then the campground obviously welcomes families enough to

provide classes and diversions for the kids.

Some campgrounds will charge for these kids' activities so if you think your children would be interested in taking part you should find out ahead of time if there is a fee for them to participate.

2. There's a pool. Anytime there is a pool you can pretty much assume there will be families there. But you should always check whether or not lifeguards are on duty all the time. Some campgrounds have lifeguards on duty only during specially designated family swims and some don't have any at all, leaving parents to be responsible for their kids' water safety.

3. There's a playground/swing set. If you see kid-friendly swings and playground equipment in the brochure or on the website, or if the person you talk with mentions that they have a playground then you can assume that the campground is kid-friendly.

4. Nearby family dining. It can be a nice break in the camping routine to go to a nice restaurant nearby that the children will like. If the campground website or promotional brochures mention family restaurants or activities nearby then it's a family friendly campground. If the campground isn't interested in having families stay there then the places they recommend will all be adult oriented so if you see a recommendation on the website or in the brochure to have dinner at "Logan's Home Style Family Restaurant" then you know you're going to be staying at a family friendly place.

5. The location of all facilities like water, community center, playground, bathrooms, and showers are in central locations that are easily accessible from any campsite. If the

distances between the campsites and the attractions are short then they are most likely going to be no problem for children.

6. There are kids or families in the photos on the website or in the promotional brochures. Do you really look at the promotional photos that are on websites and in promotional brochures? You should, because those photos can tell you a lot about a place. If you're looking at the website you should also look closely at the photos in the "gallery" section if there is one. Those photos usually are of the campsites and the grounds and if you see a lot of campsites that have families camping on them then you'll know that you and your kids will have fun there.

7. The trail maps have trails that are marked for kids. Lots of campgrounds will put their brochures and trail maps online in a .PDF format so that you can download them and look through them. When you're looking at the local hiking trails if you see some easy, flat trails that are marked as kid trails or if there is a notation that says a trail is appropriate for certain ages then you know the campground is family friendly.

8. Your friends that have children recommend it. Anytime you have a recommendation from a friend that has kids you can trust that the campground that has been recommended is family friendly. Personal recommendations are the best way to find family friendly campgrounds.

9. The community center has kid friendly DVDs and video games. Most of the time if a campground has a community center they will list on their website what types of activities are offered there like video games or DVDs. If the website doesn't specifically mention what DVDs and video games are available you should call and ask someone at the campground. If the titles are kid-appropriate then you and

your family should be fine camping there. You might want to also pack your own DVDs and games, just make sure they are clearly labeled with your name.

10. One of the amenities listed by the campground is a ball field or soccer field. If the campground is advertising the fact that it has large, open expanses of mowed grass, suitable for pick up ball games or other activities, chances are good that campground is a pretty family friendly place.

When it comes to finding a great campground that is family friendly you should also trust your gut. As a parent, you will have a pretty good sense of which campgrounds are a good place for families and which ones are more adult-oriented.

Should You Rent an RV or Use a Camping Trailer?

When you're heading off on a camping vacation one of the first things that you need to decide is whether you want to rent a recreational vehicle (RV) to use as a base of operations while you're away or if you want to rent a camping trailer that you can tow behind your car to carry all your gear. You will need something to carry all your gear in, since most people do not have a family vehicle that is large enough to carry everyone in the family and all the gear and food that you will need to bring on a camping trip.

Advantages of Renting an RV

If you don't have a lot of experience camping and don't want to stray too far from all the comforts of home but you still want to experience the joys of a family camping trip then renting an RV might be a good fit for you.

When you rent an RV you won't have to worry about the facilities or amenities that a campground has because you will have your own bathroom and shower, comfortable sleeping spaces that are protected from the weather, plus a real stove and refrigerator and sometimes even a washer and dryer too.

You can rent many different kinds of RVs from small RVs that sleep only 3-4 people and can save on gas but still give you all the comforts of home to huge RVs that cost more to drive but give you a lot of luxurious amenities and can sleep 6-8 people. If you choose to rent an RV make sure that the campground you reserve a space at has electricity and water hookups for your RV or you will be out of luck.

Renting an RV can seriously increase the amount of money that you spend on your family camping vacation but if luxury matters to you and you don't want to sleep in tents or take a chance on bad weather then you might be better off in an RV.

Additionally, if you are traveling quite a long distance to get to your destination renting an RV can save you a lot of time and money. One adult can drive while the other sleeps so that you can get to your destination faster. And you can sleep in the RV and won't need to pay for a hotel if the destination is more than a day's journey away.

If you're renting an RV then maintenance isn't a problem and you'll always have roadside support. If your RV ever breaks down or if you have an accident or another type of mechanical problem the company will send someone to come and help you or bring you a new RV, which is a big advantage of renting an RV.

When you rent an RV you will have to provide proof of a valid driver's license, insurance and other paperwork and everyone that is going to be driving the RV will need to be added to the rental contract so make sure that all the adults that are going to be driving the RV know how to drive an RV and can provide copies of a valid driver's license.

Advantages of Renting a Camping Trailer

There are several different kinds of trailers that you rent if you are not comfortable driving a big RV. The biggest advantage of any camping trailer is that they are smaller. Since they are smaller they cost less to tow and they are easier to maneuver because you can tow them with your own car or truck.

Another advantage of using a trailer that you tow with your own car is that while you are on vacation if you want to visit a local town or go out for a restaurant meal or even just go out and do some shopping you don't have to pull up stakes and drive the RV away just to run a few errands or take a quick day trip. Since you are pulling the trailer with your vehicle you can just unhitch the trailer from your vehicle and be on your way.

The most basic type of camping trailer is a trailer that is mainly used to haul gear. These trailers can cost as little as $20 per day to rent and they will give you all the extra room that you need to store tents, sleeping bags, food, extra clothes and other gear that you will need for your camping trip. If you're planning on "roughing it" then all you really need is a basic trailer to carry your gear.

If you want to have a little more comfort but you don't want to commit to renting a huge RV you can rent a travel trailer. Travel trailers are usually small enough that they can be towed by the family minivan or truck or SUV but they slide out to become a roomy home away from home. Travel trailers have some of the advantages of RVs like cozy sleeping spaces, a full kitchen, a bathroom and sometimes laundry capability as well but they are cheaper and easier to move around.

Another good option is a tent trailer or a pop up trailer. These trailers fold down flat into an easy to tow square trailer that most cars and vans can tow but they fold out and open up to a large covered space that can accommodate as many as 8 people depending on the size of the trailer. Not all of these trailers have electricity and water hooked up, some are just comfortable sleeping quarters, so double check when you're renting if you need one that has water and electricity hookups.

Pop up trailers are a great option if you have small kids that might be too easily frightened by sleeping in a tent in the great outdoors and still need to have the safety and security of feeling like they are in a secure room. Also if you are going camping in a place that has dramatic temperature drops at night you will find sleeping in a trailer a lot warmer than sleeping in a tent.

For most families that are trying to keep their camping vacation from costing a fortune but want to make sure that has everyone has a good time and is safe and happy renting a travel trailer is the best option. Driving an RV can be very difficult and the gas can be extremely expensive.

Essential Family Camping Gear

When you're taking the family out camping planning ahead is crucial. You can never plan for every situation but when you're traveling and camping with kids knowing your kids routines and finding ways to accommodate those routines within the trip can be a lifesaver and can make sure that you get some rest and relaxation too. Having the right gear, and having enough of it, is the best way to make sure that everyone is happy, feels comfortable and is safe and secure during your camping vacation.

So what gear do you really need for family camping? The most basic camping equipment that you'll need includes things like tents, stoves, day packs, backpacks, extra clothes, foods, kitchen supplies, sleeping bags, water and beverages, hiking boots, and waterproof matches.

And that's just a start. To make things more confusing you have a lot of choices when it comes to things like tents, boots and other camping clothing and sleeping bags, so even just choosing everything that you need to bring with you can be a big undertaking. And then you have to multiply that amount of gear by everyone in the family because everyone will need their own equipment and clothing.

Take a deep breath. It's really not as intimidating as it seems to choose the equipment that you're going to need. Remember you are not going to be raising your children in the woods; you're going on a family vacation that probably is not going to last more than a week, or maybe two weeks. So you don't need to stress over what the best tent is and how much it costs. Even though there is a lot of camping gear that you need to get and the cost of all that gear can add up fast you can find the essentials at different price points to accommodate any budget.

When it comes to choosing camping gear there is also some leeway in what you choose to buy depending on how you're going to camp. If you're going to be renting an RV or a travel trailer than you don't need to buy expensive all weather tents because you won't be sleeping outdoors. If you're not going to do any serious back country hiking you can probably get away with using back packs instead of day packs.

Tents

If you are going to be "roughing it" and you're not going to rent an RV or a travel trailer then you will probably end up sleeping in a tent. Since the tent is one of the most important pieces of camping equipment that you will buy when you're planning a family camping trip let's start by looking at how to find the perfect tent for you and your family.

Choosing the right tent can be tough if you're not all that familiar with camping. The first thing that you need to decide when you're picking a tent is what size tent you want. Tent sizes range from small individual tents to multi-room tents that have separate areas for sleeping, dressing, and storing gear. Multi-room tents are often recommended for family camping but they are not the right choice for every family.

Multi-Room Tents

There are advantages and disadvantages to each different type of tent and not every type of tent is going to perfect for each type of family. As a general rule you might want to consider using a multi-room tent if:

Weight doesn't matter - Multi-room tents are heavy to carry, so if you're planning on carrying your tent with you on an extended hike then you definitely don't want to get a multi-room tent. But, if you are just going to be unloading the tent from the truck to the campsite then a multi-room tent wouldn't be too heavy for you. You might want to pack a small luggage cart with wheels with your multi-room tent though, in case you have to carry your gear a long distance from your car to your campsite.

You have small children – Usually if you have kids younger than eight that are going to be camping with you and that you will need to keep a close eye on then a multi-room tent is a good choice. You and your spouse can still have a separate space in the tent away from the kids but you don't have to worry about the kids being all alone in another tent.

You have pets – Traveling with the family dog or dogs? Then definitely consider getting a multi-room tent. You probably don't want to leave your beloved family pets outside all night, or in the car, so if you have a multi-room tent you can keep the dog or dogs with you but in a separate space. That will also eliminate the problem of waking up to dog breath in your face in the middle of night or losing sleep because your dog or dogs want to sleep with you and your spouse.

You have a lot of gear and not a lot of storage space – If you are going to be camping for more than a few days you will probably end up having a lot of gear. If your family car can't hold your gear, or you need your gear to be closer to you and more accessible then using a multi-room tent can give you the extra space that you need to store your gear in a cool, dry place.

Single Room Tents

When you're buying a single room tent you will usually find tents that say they sleep two people, or four people, or even six people. But, you'll notice they don't say anything about fitting that many people in the tent comfortably. A good rule of thumb is take the number of people that the manufacturer says can sleep in the tent and divide it in half. So a two person tent would really sleep one adult comfortably, and perhaps two children. A six person tent would sleep three adults comfortably, and a few children.

Children that are older than eight or ten often like to sleep in their own tent separate from their parents so if your kids are older a couple of single room rents can be a better choice than a multi-room tent as long as you gauge the space correctly.

Tips for Figuring Out How Much Space You Need in a Tent

In order for each adult to be comfortable in a tent and to have room for personal stuff, sleeping bags, clothing and so on you need to plan on having 30 square feet per person in a tent. You might need more or less depending on the size of the people but as a general rule 30 square feet per person is the minimum amount of space that a tent should have.

So when you're choosing a basic single room tent for two adults you need to get a tent that is at least eight feet by eight feet. That comes out to 32 square feet of space per person. An eight by eight tent is also a good size for three or four kids.

Most experienced family campers agree that a 10-by-10 tent is just about perfect for two people. That gives you the space to have a double air mattress in the tent and still have enough room left over for gear. The additional height will give you the room that you need to stand up comfortably when you're getting dressed. To make things simple most families that decide to use single room tents get two tents that are the same size.

If you do choose a tent that is larger than 10-by-10 keep in mind that finding a level, even piece of ground to put your tent on that is larger than 10-by-10 might be hard depending on the campsite that you get and the terrain of the campground. If you do choose a tent that is larger than 10-by-10 you should make sure that you ask about the terrain and the size of the campsite before you reserve one.

Five Other Important Things to Consider When Choosing a Tent

Once you have decided on the type of tent that will work best for your family and the size that you need there are other things that you need to take into consideration before you purchase a tent. Make sure that you check out these five things before making a final decision about a family camping tent:

1. Shape – Tents come in several different shapes including traditional A-line, round (also called geodesic) and wall. When you're choosing the shape remember that if you do buy a round tent you will need to buy a tent that is one size larger than you think you need to accommodate for the space that you lose having a round floor.

2. What material the poles are made of – The best tent poles

are usually made of aluminum or fiberglass because they are light and easy to fix if they bend or break. Many tent poles made from aluminum or fiberglass come with repair kits so that if they do bend or break they will be easy to fix.

3. The fabric that the tent is made from – Almost all tents are made of nylon, but higher quality tents will use thick nylon or rip stop fabric instead of basic nylon. A good tent should have an outer shell made of waterproofed nylon and should have a nylon mesh inner lining to help with air flow and to keep bugs out.

4. The zippers – Always double check the zippers before you buy a tent to make sure that they function properly and that they slide easily. The zippers should be set into the tent securely with no fraying or loosening. The zippers should also be made of a rust proof material so check the product specifications if you're not sure they are.

5. The seams- The seams on a tent are very important. All the seams on a high quality tent will be reinforced with nylon tape. The nylon tape should be sewn into every seam to help make it more waterproof. The tent should also come with a tube of seam sealant that you will need to apply every year before you go out camping.

Because the seams on your tent are so important you should set up the tent at home before you go camping and turn the hose on it, stretch it, take it down and put it up several times, leave it in the sun for a few hours and do everything else that you would do to the tent on an actual camping trip to it. Then see how well the seams are holding up. If you see any fraying or notice the seams ripping or weakening then take the tent back and get another.

Your tent is an essential piece of camping gear so it pays to take some time, do some research, and make sure that you pick the right one for your family.

Packs

Choosing the right pack to carry your gear and the items that you will need to take on a hike with you is more important for the teenagers and adults in your family than the little ones. If your little ones want to help carry items on a hike then a high quality children's backpack, like the ones they use for school, should be just fine.

You can put rain gear, extra socks, a sweater and a water bottle in their backpacks and they will be all set. You and the older children will end up carrying most of the gear so the packs that you choose will make a big difference in whether or not you have a great hike or a miserable one. The first thing that you need to decide when you're choosing a pack is whether you want an internal frame pack or an external frame pack.

Internal Frame Packs

Internal frame packs were originally designed to be used by rock climbers that needed a pack that was more flexible and hugged the body more closely than the traditional external frame pack. Internal frame packs leave your arms freer and make movement easier and also don't pull to one side or another. They are taller and narrower than external frame packs. Internal frame packs are often recommended for hiking and skiing or horseback riding treks. They have become a very popular type of backpack for these reasons.

One of the biggest advantages of using an internal frame pack is that they are extremely flexible and follow the motion of your back so if you're going to be heading off on a long hike you might find that an internal frame pack is more comfortable because it has so much more flexibility.

For parents hiking with kids the extra stability of an internal frame pack is great just in case you need to pick up and carry a child along with your pack. Also, since your arms will be under less pressure and stress you will have a hand available to help a child over a rough spot in the trail or hold a hand while crossing a stream if you need to.

There are a few disadvantages of using internal frame packs though. Because the pack sits much closer to your body and follows the shape of your back you will sweat more because there won't be as much air flow as there would be with an external frame pack. Another disadvantage is that internal frame packs usually don't have a lot of outside pockets and pouches. Most of your gear will need to be packed into the center compartment of the pack which might make it harder to get at if you need it.

External Frame Packs

External frame packs have been the choice of hikers and

campers for many years. External frame packs can be up to three pounds lighter than an internal frame pack and when you're carrying a lot of gear, snacks, and sometimes even a small child that three pounds can make a big difference.

The other big advantages that an external pack has is that the pack fits further away from your body so you will get some air flow between your back and the pack which help keep you from getting hot and sweaty when you're hiking. The external frame pack also is more rigid and distributes the weight of the pack differently so that instead of carrying the bulk of the weight of the pack on your shoulders you're actually carrying it on your hips.

Some of the disadvantages of external frame packs are that they have lots of outside pockets and pouches that can get snagged on trees or rocks and pull you off balance or rip the pack. External frame packs are also very rigid which makes it difficult to climb or hike a difficult trail while wearing one. External frame packs don't move with your body and that can be painful if you're going to be wearing the pack for a long period of time.

Choosing the Right Pack

Once you have decided whether or not you want an internal frame pack or an external frame pack you will need to choose the size of your pack. Here is a brief overview of the most common sizes of packs and how much gear they hold so that you can make an informed decision about what size pack will be the best one for you:

Half day packs

Half day packs are fairly small and can only really carry the essentials like water, a lunch or a snack, dry socks, rain gear, an extra jacket or sweater and a first aid kit. If you're going for a short hike with the kids or if you're not going very far from your campsite then this size pack will be ideal.

Full day packs

Full day packs are more substantial and are the perfect choice for a full day of hiking or if you have to carry gear for yourself and your family. These packs come with waist straps and other support plus external loops and straps to hold a GPS navigator, water bottles, lunches, and other necessary items that you want to be able to reach quickly. Inside there is plenty of space to keep all the extras that you need to take with you for everyone in the family.

Multi-day packs

In general if you're not going on a full hiking trip where you are carrying tents and all your equipment with you then you won't need a pack bigger than a full day pack. But if you are ambitious and are planning a full back country hiking vacation where you'll be carrying all of your gear with you then you will definitely need a multi-day pack.

Camping Stoves

When you're camping with the family you will definitely need a two burner or even a three burner camping stove. The little one burner stoves are great for when you're camping alone but if you have a family to feed it's a lot faster and more economical to use a larger stove so that you can cook real meals.

There are lots of different styles and sizes of camping stoves that you can choose from but the most important thing to consider when you're choosing a camping stove is what type of fuel the stove runs on. Experienced family campers agree that there are really only two decent choices when it comes to camping stoves that are appropriate for family camping: propane or white gas.

Propane Camping Stoves

Propane camping stoves are by far the most popular choice. This is due to several advantages that propane stoves have over other stoves. The first big advantage of using a propane stove is that with propane stoves there is no risk of fuel spilling. That is very important when you have small kids running around. Propane stoves operate on either small cans of propane that fit directly into the stove or through propane from a large tank through a hose fixed securely to the stove.

Propane stoves are easier to start than other types of camping stoves. Some propane stoves even have electric starters so that you don't even have to light the stove. When you have kids running around having an electric starting stove can be a lot safer than using a stove that needs to be lit. Another advantage of propane is that it's relatively inexpensive and it's easy to find.

Families that haven't been on too many family camping trips usually find that using a propane stove is the closest thing to their "normal" family routine and that can make the kids feel more secure while making it easier for the parents to adjust to the challenges of cooking outdoors instead of cooking in the kitchen at home.

Propane doesn't give out as much heat as some of the other types of fuel, so that might be a disadvantage but usually most people don't consider that to be too much of a problem. Families that go camping a lot report that the advantages of using a propane stove far outweigh the few disadvantages of using a propone stove so when you're choosing a camping stove you definitely need to consider a propane stove.

If you don't want to use a propane stove then the next best option according to experienced family campers is a white gas stove.

White Gas Stoves

The biggest advantage of using white gas stoves campers say is that it leaves no fuel odor on your hands or clothes if you spill it, and there's no odor or weird taste to your food. White gas stoves burn the hottest of any type of camping stove so if you want a stove capable of hitting very high temperatures than you might to choose a white gas stove.

If you're considering buying a white gas stove you should get a special type of white gas stove known as a duel fuel stove. This stove can be run with white gas, or with a little unleaded gasoline, the same kind that you put in your car. The advantage of a duel fuel stove is that if you run out of white gas you can use regular unleaded gas from the gas station to fuel your stove.

White gas stoves are extremely reliable and since the white gas is a clean fuel you rarely need to clean the stove or disassemble it the way you need to do with a propane stove. White gas stoves are also cost effective because they will last for years with very little maintenance.

The biggest disadvantage of using white gas stove is that the fuel needs to be physically poured from the bottle into the fuel tube of the stove, which can lead to spills. But since the fuel evaporates fast and doesn't have an odor even if you spill some you won't smell like gas.

The lack of odor can be a problem though, because if there is a fuel leak you won't smell anything and might not know. It's not a big problem if the fuel leaks onto your clothes or into your tent because it will evaporate but if the fuel leaks into your food storage container even if the fuel evaporates your food could be ruined.

Another disadvantage of using a white gas stove is that the high heat makes it difficult to cook some items that need to be cooked over a low flame or simmered for a long time. You may not be able to cook with the same kind of finesse that you're used to when you're cooking with a white gas stove and you might need to adjust your recipes accordingly.

White gas stoves are usually lighter than propane stoves and thus are often the preference of wilderness hikers who are roughing it across long distances. For most campers though, unless you are planning on carrying the stove on a long hike with you or if you are backpacking and you are carrying all your gear with you then the weight of the stove usually isn't that large of a consideration when choosing a type of stove.

Ultimately no matter type of stove you choose to take with you on your family camping trip the first consideration should always be safety. They are potentially quite dangerous. You should always be careful when you are using a camping stove around children.

Lanterns

Lanterns and flashlights are something that every family will need on a family camping trip. You can pretty much count on having to leave a lit lantern as a "night light" in the kids' tent if your kids are young, and there should always be a lantern around for someone to take to the bathroom in the middle of the night. So what type of lantern is the best to take on a family camping vacation? Here's a brief look at your choices:

Solar powered

Solar powered lanterns are a great choice for family vacations because you won't have to worry about a battery dying in the middle of the night or having the kids around fuel like gas or propane. It is also the most environmentally friendly and non-toxic lantern option. The biggest problem with solar lanterns is that if the day is not sunny then you won't have a working lantern at night. If you're going to rely on solar lanterns make sure the weather forecast says sun or bring a battery backup.

Battery powered

Battery powered lanterns are also a great choice for family camping because they are safe, easy to use, and won't run out of power unless you forget to bring the backup batteries. The biggest disadvantage of using battery powered lanterns is the cost of the batteries. When you're packing for your family camping trip if you're using battery powered lanterns always get at least twice as many batteries as you think you'll need, just in case you can't find batteries when you're out camping.

If you are worried about the cost of the batteries you can get rechargeable battery lanterns and you can plug the charger into your car battery to get enough power to recharge all the lantern batteries.

Gas powered lanterns

Though traditionally used, generally gas powered lanterns are not a good choice when you're camping with kids. Gas powered lanterns are dangerous – they can tip over and spill fuel or even start a fire. Any type of liquid fuel lantern is generally not recommended for family camping. Stick with battery or solar powered lanterns to make sure that everyone stays safe.

There is another alternative when it comes to camping lights. For kids that are scared of the dark and want a night light in their tents or don't feel comfortable walking around with a lantern but don't want to be in the dark stick glow sticks are great. The same glow sticks that are used to light up the night for kids at Halloween can be the perfect camping accessory. They burn for hours without getting hot and will eventually go out on their own.

Glow sticks are cheap, and you can get hundreds of them in many different colors for under $50. Look online or in party supply shops to find them in the spring and the summer. Glow stick bracelets, necklaces and anklets are also a fun alternative.

Sleeping Bags and Mattresses

When you're out camping you can sleep in a sleeping bag on a groundsheet or pad or you can use an air mattress. Air mattresses are the choice of most family campers because they are more comfortable and they make kids feel more at home and like they are sleeping in their own beds.

If you're using an air mattress buy one that has a self pump to make sure that you are always able to inflate it. Air mattresses run the gamut when it comes to prices. You can get a cheap twin size air mattress for less than $20 or you can buy a top of the line king size air mattress that costs hundreds of dollars.

Sleeping bags are more commonly used by people that are carrying all their gear with them and backpacking instead of staying at a fixed campsite. But, kids can really enjoy the experience of camping out and sleeping in their sleeping bags. A sleeping bag can also be a great way to stay warm, because many national parks and other camping destinations get quite cool at night even in the middle of the summer.

Here are some tips for buying sleeping bags for your family camping trip:

- There are three main shapes of sleeping bag. Mummy shaped bags are shaped in an inverted triangle with the widest points across the shoulders and a narrow V for your feet the bottom. Some people love the cozy feeling of being in a mummy shaped bag, but some people hate it. You can also choose a semi-rectangular bag that is more square in shape but has a narrow V at the bottom a rectangular bag which is a traditional rectangle shape.

- Look for a sleeping bag with an insulated draft collar to keep the cold and damp off your neck and shoulders

- Make sure the bag has a wind proof and weather resistant outer shell.

- A three season bag is all that most people need. A three season bag will keep you warm in temperatures about 20 degrees above zero and it rarely get colder than that when you're camping in the summer.

- Look for a sleeping bag that has a lining of taffeta or another non cotton material. Non cotton materials will breathe better, warm up more quickly, and stay warm longer.

- Look for a sleeping bag that has a fleece lined carrying pouch. Then you can turn the carrying pouch inside out and use that for a cozy pillow at night.

- If you want a sleeping bag that you and your spouse can share or if you want to sleep inside a sleeping bag on top of an air mattress get two rectangle shaped sleeping bags, unfold them and zip them together.

- If you don't use an air mattress you should always use a ground pad. A foam core high density pad will give you the most padding.

- Down filled sleeping bags give the most warmth, but if they get wet they are useless, so if there any chance that your bags will get wet choose a bag with a synthetic filling instead.

- Always try out your sleeping bags thoroughly before you go camping. You might feel stupid in the store zipping yourself into a sleeping bag but you should always get into the bag, zip it, move around in it, roll around in it and really test it for comfort and durability before you buy.

- If you are buying a sleeping bag for a baby or toddler check to make sure it has proper ventilation. Babies can easily get overheated if the sleeping bag is not properly ventilated.

- You should buy an additional sleeping bag liner if your bag doesn't come with one. This will help keep your warmer and it will help keep the bag clean because you can remove the liner and wash it instead of trying to clean the whole bag.

Five Ways to Get Great Deals on Camping Gear

Buying all the camping gear that you need to have for everyone in the family can get very expensive, very quickly. If this is your first family camping trip then you probably don't want to spend thousands of dollars on new high end camping equipment until you for sure that family camping trips are something that you'll be doing more in the future.

How can you get the gear that you and your family need without spending a small fortune? Here are five ways to find everything you need for less:

1. Borrow it – Do you have friends that go camping with their kids? Or do you family that have gone camping in the past or maybe you have some friends that are outdoor enthusiasts?

Borrow anything you can from them. Borrow lanterns, sleeping bags, a stove, whatever they have. Anything that you don't have to buy is money saved.

2. Rent it - Not all of the camping gear that you need to have will be available for rental but some camping and outdoor sports stores like REI do rent things like tents and stoves and other large pieces of camping equipment. Since those are the things that you would end up spending the biggest amount of money on it makes sense to see if you can rent those things instead of buying. Check with your local sporting goods and outdoor sports stores to see what equipment they rent.

3. Buy second hand – Scour local resale shops or used sporting goods stores for second hand camping gear that is still in good condition. Chances are pretty good that you will find some great gear that has only been used once that was purchased by other family campers who decided camping wasn't for them. You should probably not buy used sleeping bags, but other second hand equipment could save you lots money. You can also take your chances at garage sales and yard sales.

4. Equipment swaps – Do your kids play sports and have a lot of old sports gear? Look for local sports equipment swaps to see if you can trade your kids' old, outgrown gear for some family camping gear. Many times local community sports leagues, sporting teams, Boy Scout and Girl Scout groups and other community groups will hold equipment swaps. Check with your local parks department to find equipment swaps in your area.

5. Look online – Scour sites like Craigslist or Freecycle to find free or low cost camping equipment that is still in good condition. Sometimes you can get amazing deals on

equipment that is practically new when you look on the Internet.

What to Do if You or Your Kids Take Daily Medications

Sometimes parents that have kids who are on behavioral medications or other types of daily meds think that they can give the kids a rest when they go on vacation and not give them their medication. Taking a child off medication suddenly can have very serious consequences so experts recommend that you keep the kids on their daily medication schedule. Here are some tips to make it easier to keep your kids, or you and your spouse, on a daily medication schedule even when you're on vacation:

- Call the doctor that prescribed the medication and get an extra prescription. Take one bottle of pills with you and leave one at home. That way if the bottle that you bring on vacation gets lost or thrown away you will already have some at home and won't need to call the doctor panicking because the pills are gone. Most doctors will accommodate you by giving you another prescription or allowing you another refill if you explain why you need it.

- Use a daily pill container. Those little pill holders that most drug stores give away aren't just for the elderly. They are a fantastic way to keep vitamins and medications dry and safe on a camping trip. Use a separate pill holder for each person in the family. Clearly label the holders with the person's name too so that there is no confusing.

- Set a reminder alarm. Use the alarm feature on your cell phone or watches as a reminder to you and the kids when the medicines need to be taken. Carry a bottle of water with you all the time so that even if you're in the middle of a hike you or one of the kids can take medicine if needed.

- Keep a separate pill container filled with over the counter medicines. To make sure that no one takes the wrong pill by mistake use a separate pill holder that is clearly labeled "OTC" to hold medications like ibuprofen or other pain relievers, heartburn pills, allergy pills, sinus pills, or other over the counter medications that you might need while you're on vacation.

- Find the nearest local pharmacy. Even though you're going to be camping out in the wilderness you will probably never be more than a few hours trip to a town that has a pharmacy or hospital. Before you go on your trip use the Internet to find the address and phone number of the closest pharmacy to where you will be camping.

Program the phone number into your cell phone, and write down the address and phone number on a little card and put that in your wallet. That way if you need to call there to get a prescription refilled or if you need to go there in a hurry you'll have the address and phone number right at your fingertips.

What you Need to Have in a Well Stocked First Aid Kit

When you go camping with kids you cannot have too many first aid supplies. Of course you hope that during the course of the trip no one will get any injuries and that everything will go smoothly but that rarely happens. Injuries might be small scratches, bug bites, and bruised knees or they could be serious cuts, sprains or even a broken bone or burns from a campfire.

When you're out in the wilderness camping you might be several miles or several hours from any kind of medical help so having enough first aid supplies to at least stabilize and begin treatment of an injured person is crucial. You might think that you don't really need all of these first aid supplies but if a situation comes up and you don't have them you will regret not having a well stocked first aid it.

You can buy pre-assembled kits from camping stores but many families prefer to make their own kits because then they can personalize them with items that are specific to their kids and spouse. A pre-assembled kit is a good place to start and will give you a lot of the basics that you need, so you might want to buy a pre-assembled kit and just add to it.

Expert family campers say it's cheaper in the long run to stock your own kit from scratch however because you get more materials that way.

When you go camping with kids you will need to have several first aid kids. You will need one large, main first aid kit that has the bulk of the first aid supplies but each child should also have their own individual first aid kit that they can carry with them. Pre-assembled kits are fine for kids' first aid packs. They usually contain bandages and gauze for small cuts and scraped, calamine lotion, antibiotic cream and Q tips. Add to that some bug spray, sunscreen, and hand sanitizer and that should be fine.

But when it comes to stocking the big first aid kit you're going to need a little more than that. The first thing that you need to do is get a container for your first aid kit. You can buy a first aid box in some specialty stores but a cheap alternative is a plastic tackle box. A plastic tackle box will be lightweight, durable, waterproof, and will have lots of room inside for all your supplies.

Once you have your tackle box to store all your first aid supplies then it's time to go shopping. Check out discount pharmacies or medical supply warehouses and even discount stores to get the best price possible on these essential first aid supplies.

To make shopping easier you can just print out this list and take it to the store with you:

Essential First Aid Supplies

- Band Aids- Get some 'kid friendly' ones in fun colors or patterns. Also get several different kinds and sizes like butterfly or knuckle bandages.

- Gauze Pads – Get several sizes

- Gauze – Several rolls in different sizes

- Bandage tape

- Duct tape

- Electrical tape

- Sanitary napkins or diapers (great for stopping the bleeding of large cuts or wounds)

- Vet Wrap – Vet Wrap is a nice waterproof alternative to tape. Plus it comes in fun colors and can be used as a brace as well.

- Scissors

- Razor

- Moleskin

- Water Purifying Tablets

- Antiseptic Ointment

- Ace Bandages

- Calamine Lotion

- Baking Soda

- Diarrhea medicine

- Cold and sinus medicines

- Cough/Throat Lozenges

- Ibuprofen or pain relievers

- Mirror
- Hand Sanitizer
- Baby wipes
- Tweezers
- Antiseptic Wipes
- Eyewash
- Aloe Vera gel
- Disinfectant Soap
- Latex Gloves
- CPR Breathing Mask
- Ipecac
- Charcoal Tablets
- Sewing Needles
- Thread
- Hydrogen Peroxide
- Cold and hot packs
- Snake bite kit
- Epi pen for anyone that is allergic to things like bees
- Avon Skin So Soft or another bug repellant
- Bulb irrigating syringes
- Antihistamines
- Antacid
- Safety pins
- A card with any medical conditions that your family has written on it
- The name and phone number of your doctor and pharmacy and emergency contact

- A disposable cell phone that has pre-programmed phone numbers for your doctor, the park ranger station or the office at the campground, the nearest hospital, and your emergency contact. Teach the kids how to use the pre-sets so that if something happened to you they could call for help.

- Emergency flares

- Sunscreen

You can also put in your own medications that you take daily to make sure that they stay in a safe, dry place. The good news is that you will probably only have to buy these materials once. Each year before you go camping go through the first aid kit and replace anything that is outdated or has been used already.

A good way to keep track of what you have is to print out that list and keep a copy in the box as an inventory list. Then if you use an item from the list cross it off and you will know what items need replacing without having to dig through the whole kit.

Basic First Aid Tips

Cuts and scraped usually don't need that much attention. When your children get cuts and scrapes don't make a big production over it or you will just scare them. Wash the cut with soap and water, or use an antibacterial wipe if you're not near any water, put some antibiotic cream on it and bandage it.

Sunburn can be more serious than you think. Put hats on the kids and plenty of sunscreen. Be careful to guard yourself from the sun too. If sunburn does occur treat it with pure Aloe Vera gel, some ibuprofen, and cold packs.

Sunstroke or heatstroke is a real danger when you're hiking. Rest frequently, especially if you have kids with you, and make sure that everyone drinks plenty of water. You might want to use a mixture of half sports drinks and half water to help the kids stay properly hydrated. Cutting the sports drinks with water will help cut down on their sugar intake.

Take sprains seriously. The person with the sprain should rest as much as possible and elevate the sprained area and use a cold pack to reduce swelling.

traditional camping foods for your family camping trip

Kids are notoriously hard to please when it comes to food, and getting them to try new foods can be challenging. So when planning your menu for your camping trip try to pick foods that you have all the time at home that you can cook at a campsite. If you have a two burner stove you can make just about any dish that you make at home, although there are some foods that are traditionally associated with camping that can be fun to make for the family.

Try making some of these camping classics with your kids to make your family camping trip more fun:

Trail mix – No camping trip would be complete with this staple snack. Trail mix can be bought in a prepared form in bulk at most natural foods stores or health food stores or you can make your own. To make your own mix your favorite nuts, pretzels, dried fruit and dried cereal in a big container and shake it. Make a lot of it because this snack is perfect for camping and everyone will be munching it.

S'mores – You have to make s'mores on a family camping trip. Chocolate, marshmallows and graham crackers are all you need. You can use regular milk chocolate or add your favorite variation. Dark chocolate, low fat chocolate, sugar free chocolate, there are endless possibilities. Making these treats with your kids will be something you and they will always remember.

Toasted marshmallows – Bring lots of marshmallows because you will need them for s'mores and you will need them for toasting and roasting. No family camping trip would be complete without a few evenings spent around a roaring campfire toasting marshmallows.

Foil packs – Foil packs are great for camping because they are easy to make, easy to clean up, and they are something that most people only make on camping trips. To make a foil pack just put all the items you want to make in your meal in one large sheet of foil, cover it with more foil and stick it in the coals and let it cook. Foil packs are great for cooking potatoes and vegetables.

Toast on a stick – Let the kids make their own breakfast over a campfire by placing pieces of bread on skewers and holding it over a fire until it's perfectly toasted. Chances are good that your kids will be enthralled, even if it takes a few tries to get the bread toasted just right.

These are just a few classic camping meals that most people enjoy. You can make your own traditions by coming up with your own family camping recipes that you and your kids can make while you're camping.

Creating a tradition of making certain foods on family camping trips is something that your kids will always remember and will pass on to their kids too.

Family Camping Cooking Tips

Trying to plan a menu and shop for enough food to keep everyone happy and well fed during the entire vacation can be a daunting task. Here are some tips that can make it easier:

- Plan a menu and stick to it. That will make shopping and cooking much, much easier. Just make sure that you buy enough food and snacks.

- As a general rule buy twice as much of everything as you think you will need. If you don't use it all you can use it at home but if you need it on your family camping trip at least you'll have it.

- Buy two or three large (30 gallon) plastic storage totes with lids. These are ideal for holding food. The containers are waterproof and airtight and will protect your food from the elements, critters, and spoiling. You will also need a few large coolers.

- Use block ice in your coolers instead of cubed. Block ice lasts longer and will result in less mess.

- Buy some bread and peanut butter, ramen noodles, or mac and cheese as a fast, easy meal alternative to whatever meal you have planned. That will also give fussy eaters an option if they don't want to eat what you've cooked.

- Cook as many things as you can ahead of time. It's much easier to reheat something than to cook it from scratch so anything that will travel and keep well cook before you leave. Pre-cooked meats are much safer than raw meats so cook your meat ahead or buy a of pre-cooked deli meat.

- Buy a set of durable plastic dishes for camping. You can get these at any home store for just a few dollars. Get two sets of everything that you will need.

- You cannot have too many waterproof kitchen matches. Use the plastic from your food containers to keep the matches dry.

- Buy a coffee percolator if you're a coffee drinker. A coffee percolator is a great way to make coffee on a campfire.

- You will need a lot of plastic wrap and aluminum foil so buy plenty of both. Aluminum foil is great for cooking and the plastic wrap will help store leftovers.

- Don't forget the dish soap and sponges to wash your plastic dishes and cooking utensils.

- Bring several plastic cutting boards. There are usually not that many clean places to prepare food on a campsite and picnic tables can be very difficult to prepare food on.

- Bring two manual can openers and two bottle openers.

- Measure out the ingredients that you'll need for cooking ahead of time and store them in plastic air tight bags. A great way to keep your meal ingredients organized is to buy small plastic totes with lids, shoebox size ones, and put all the ingredients for one meal in one tote. Label the lid and you can just pull out that tote when you want to make that meal and have all the ingredients at your fingertips.

- Make sure your sharp knives for cooking are well sheathed in hard containers and kept away from the kids.

- Use metal measure cups because they won't melt if you get them too close to the fire and won't break. Don't bring glass anything – it is just asking for trouble.

- Freeze your meals before you leave home and then they will slowly thaw through the course of your trip. That will make them last longer and also help keep other food cooler.

- Don't forget pot holders or oven mitts.

- Always supervise your kids when they are helping you cook.

- Make sure you throw away your trash and keep your food away from the campsite if you're in an area that has bears. If you have plastic totes of food keep them locked in your car away from your tents. Never keep food in the tents, not even a snack.

- Make hearty meals. When you're outdoors hiking and the kids are playing outdoors all day you will all probably be hungrier than normal. A nice chicken salad might be a great dinner at home but when you're on a camping vacation everyone will appreciate hearty, filling meals.

- Use old film containers to hold your matches. They will keep the matches from being lost and keep them dry.

- Let the kids help. They can toast bread, roast vegetables or help you prepare the food in other ways. Campfire cooking is fun and it's part of the experience of a family camping trip. You're not on a schedule when you're camping so it doesn't matter if it takes 45 minutes to make dinner because the kids are helping. Supervise them closely, but let them help.

Five Easy Tasks Around the Campsite the Kids Can Help You With

By the time you get the kids to the campsite they will probably be cranky, bored, and more than ready to get out of the car and run around. But you need to keep an eye on them and set up your campsite. The simple solution is to have the kids help you set up the campsite and unpack the gear.

The trick to getting your kids to help is to give them tasks that they can easy accomplish so that they don't get frustrated and give up and to make setting up the campsite seem like a game. Here are five easy tasks that kids can do to help set up the campsite:

1. Gather firewood – This is a great way to get them out of the car and active but still keep them relatively nearby. Show them what type of sticks are the best for building a fire and turn them loose to gather firewood. Make it a game to see who can gather the most firewood with a prize for the winner to be awarded over the campfire that night.

2. Set up tents – Depending on the child's age an adult might

have to put up the actual tent poles but the kids can work on smoothing out the tent sides, weighing down the edges and making sure all the zippers are zipped correctly. Seems there is always a need for another set of hands to hold or steady something when setting up the tents.

3. Carrying stuff from the car – This is usually not a very fun task, but if you make it a game to see who can carry more stuff, or how fast you can all get the car unloaded it will be more fun and it will helpful. This might not work on older kids who will know you're just trying to get them to help unload stuff from the car but the little ones might still fall for it.

4. Unrolling sleeping bags and blowing up air mattresses – Let the kids set up their own tents and then unpack their sleeping bags or blow up their air mattresses. Since staying in a tent is not something they get to do everyday they will probably have a lot of fun getting their tent set up just the way they want it. And if they're setting up their tents you'll know exactly where they are and it will be easy to keep an eye on them.

5. Preparing the next meal- Let the kids help unpack the food and get all the stuff ready to cook the next meal. They can help you with cooking or assembling sandwiches, put a tablecloth on the picnic table, set the table, and help carry items to the table.

There are also lots of other tasks that kids can help with when you're setting up the campsite so make sure that you let them help. Part of the fun of a family camping trip is getting to spend some quality time with your kids so don't focus only on getting a task done, focus on how it gets done. It's ok if it takes awhile. It's more important that you get to spend some one on one time with your kids.

Five Tips for Hiking with Kids

Hiking with kids is a lot different than hiking on your own. When you're hiking with kids the focus shouldn't be on the destination but on the journey. Take time along the way to notice the wildlife and natural landscape. Let the kids play around and don't be so concerned about reaching a certain point along the trail that you forget that you are all there to have fun. Use these five tips to make hiking with kids a little easier and a lot more fun:

1. Lower your expectations – Depending on how young your kids are you might not even hike a mile even if you're out hiking for a whole morning. Kids do things on their own schedules and of course can't walk as far or as fast. Be willing to let go of your goal to reach a certain destination and just go for a walk in the woods or the fields with your kids.

2. Choose appropriate trails – Choose short, easy trails when you're hiking with kids. Kids are not going to be able to handle high elevations or difficult climbs so make sure that you use trails that are marked for beginners or marked as being appropriate for kids. Pick trails that have a lot of wildlife or that have ponds, lakes, forests or large open fields so that the kids will have lots of things to look at and explore.

3. Rest a lot – Take breaks every 10 or 15 minutes. Kids get tired a lot faster than adults and they will need to stop and take a breather more frequently than you. When you stop to take a quick rest encourage them to drink water or sports

drinks so they don't get dehydrated. Take advantage of these rest breaks and use them as a time to point out certain flowers or talk about the wildlife in the area.

4. Bring extra clothes – Kids get cold a lot faster than adults, especially if they're wet. In a matter of seconds a child can go from safely exploring the edge of a pond or stream to being soaking wet. Keep an extra set of clothes, a jacket or sweater, and at least two pairs of dry socks in your pack for your child.

You should also keep an extra hat for your child, sunscreen, and plenty of water or sports drinks in your pack so that your child won't get heatstroke, get badly sunburned, or get dehydrated during the course of the hike.

5. Look for educational opportunities – There's no better place to teach your children about science and the natural world then out in the natural world. Be patient and flexible and embrace opportunities to teach your kids about nature as they come up. For example if a turtle crosses the path in front of you take the time to watch the turtle for awhile and teach your children about turtles.

Or if you see animal tracks in the dirt show your child the tracks and try to figure out what animal made the tracks. Part of the joy of a family camping vacation is experiencing the natural world together. Don't miss out on that.

Five Ways to Keep the Kids Busy if the Weather Turns Bad

Whenever you go on family camping trip you hope and pray that the weather will hold out and be sunny and warm but that won't always happen. You might run into cold, damp, rainy weather that will make keeping the kids occupied a challenge. The key to handling bad weather on a camping trip is to be prepared. Plan games and activities ahead of time so that if the weather does turn bad or if the kids are just too hot and tired to go hiking and want some down time. Here are five ways that you can keep the kids from getting bored if the weather gets bad:

1. Arts and crafts – Kids love to make arts and crafts, and you have a whole world of supplies at your fingertips when you're in the outdoors. Plan ahead and pack a storage tote full of things like glue, papers, scissors, sparkles, pens and pencils, chalk, crayons, and other arts and crafts gear. You can have the kids do crafts in their tent if the weather is really nasty or if your campsite has a covered picnic table or pavilion let them do the crafts there.

2. Tell stories – This is a fun way to get some real quality time with your kids. Have everyone curl up on their sleeping bags in one tent and tell stories. When you get tired of talking have the kids make up a story to tell you. Kids love stories and a rainy afternoon of story time with a parent will be something your kids will always remember.

3. A paper bag puppet show – Make sure that you pack paper lunch bags, felt and glue and your can kids can put on a paper bag puppet show. Have them come up with an idea, then make the puppets for the show and practice how they

want the show to go. Then let them put on the puppet show later that night.

4. Enjoy the rain – Put the kids' rain gear on them and send them out to splash in puddles and play in the rain. Kids love to play in the rain and at home chances are that they don't get to very often. Just be waiting with warm, dry clothes and a warm cup of hot chocolate when they're done splashing around to make sure that they get warm and dry quickly.

5. Organize activities with other families – If the weather is bad then the entire campground is probably full of kids that have nothing to do. You could take your kids to visit the other campsites and say hi to everyone and see if the other kids would like to do arts and crafts with your kids, or help with the puppet show.

If the campground has a community center you could set up arts and crafts for all the kids to do or you could organize some indoor games in the community center. The key to keeping kids busy during bad weather is to be creative and plan ahead.

Conclusion

A family camping trip can be a wonderful way to spend some quality time with your children and your spouse. Nothing brings a family together like simple outdoor activities, campfires, and being out together in nature. Family camping trips are also a great way to teach your kids about nature and to show them beautiful national parks and historic sites.

Planning a family camping trip can be tough and intimidating at first. It requires a lot of planning and a lot of organization but once you have gone on a couple of family camping trips and have figured out an organizational system that works well for your and your family it will be a lot easier to get ready for family camping trips. As they get older the kids can help you plan and can suggest places to go camping.

Family camping trips can be significantly cheaper than many other types of vacations, especially if you have a large family. With the cost of living rising rapidly more and more families are cutting out vacations altogether but you can still have an affordable vacation that gives you a lot of time to spend with your family if you go on a camping vacation.

The ideas in this book should help you get started planning where to go, figuring out what camping gear you need, and what you need to buy to take with you on your trip. Family camping is something that your kids will remember all their lives and the shared experiences of a family camping trip can help strengthen your family bond.

Good luck to you as you start planning a family camping vacation!

7366817R0

Made in the USA
Lexington, KY
28 November 2010